MW00719759

ESSENTIAL CONCEPTS IN COMPUTER SCIENCE

USING PSEUDOCODE

INSTRUCTIONS IN PLAIN ENGLISH

JONATHAN BARD

PowerKiDS
press™

New York

Published in 2019 by The Rosen Publishing Group, Inc.
29 East 21st Street, New York, NY 10010

First Edition

Editor: Jane Katirgis
Book Design: Reann Nye

Photo Credits: Cover cobalt88/Shutterstock.com; pp. 4, 15 BEST-BACKGROUNDS/Shutterstock.com; p. 5 Jet Cat Studio/Shutterstock.com; p. 7 Hero Images/Getty Images; p. 9 Bounce/Cultura/Getty Images; p. 11 Werner Heiber/Shutterstock.com; p. 12 TijanaM/Shutterstock.com; p. 13 Tetra Images/Getty Images; p. 17 Bobicova Valeria/Shutterstock.com; p. 18 PR Image Factory/Shutterstock.com; p. 19 REDPIXEL.PL/Shutterstock.com; p. 20 https://commons.wikimedia.org/wiki/File:Margaret_Hamilton_-_restoration.jpg; p. 21 nd3000/Shutterstock.com; p. 23 Aila Images/Shutterstock.com; p. 25 Caiaimage/Agnieszka Olek/Caiaimage/Getty Images; p. 27 Goran Bogicevic/Shutterstock.com; p. 28 https://commons.wikimedia.org/wiki/File:FloorGoban.JPG; p. 29 Klaus Vedfelt/Taxi/Getty Images; p. 30 arabianEye/Getty Images.

Cataloging-in-Publication Data

Names: Bard, Jonathan.
Title: Using pseudocode / Jonathan Bard.
Description: New York : PowerKids Press, 2019. | Series: Essential concepts in computer science | Includes glossary and index.
Identifers: LCCN ISBN 9781538331781 (pbk.) | ISBN 9781538331774 (library bound) | ISBN 9781538331798 (6 pack)
Subjects: LCSH: Pseudocode (Computer program language)–Juvenile literature. | Computer algorithms–Juvenile literature.
Classifcation: LCC QA76.73.P79 B37 2019 | DDC 005.1–dc23

Manufactured in the United States of America

CPSIA Compliance Information: Batch #CS18PK: For Further Information contact Rosen Publishing, New York, New York at 1-800-237-9932

CONTENTS

CODE IS ALL AROUND US

Code is behind every kind of device, including phones, computers, televisions, and even cars. Code is a set of instructions a device uses to function. For example, if you make a phone call, code connects you to the person you're calling. Programmers carefully plan and write this code in **coding languages**. A coding language is a lot like other languages you've heard of, such as English, Spanish, or Chinese. However, people don't

CODING LANGUAGES

There are hundreds, maybe even thousands, of programming languages used every day around the world. Some languages, such as Java, C, Python, and Perl, are extremely popular. But every year, new languages are developed, and some quickly become favorites. For example, Apple's Swift language is only a few years old, but it's already widely used. Meanwhile, C has been around for almost fifty years.

Code makes it possible to talk, text, and video chat on different devices with people nearby or very far away. Each task you want your phone, tablet, or computer to do requires unique code in order to work.

speak it, and computers can understand it.

Before they write any code, groups of programmers meet and plan every detail of the project. It can take months or years before they start writing any real code. During the planning stage, programmers write in **pseudocode**. Pseudocode is written in whatever language the programmers speak, such as plain English.

REQUIREMENTS

Before any code or pseudocode can be written, programmers must understand what the program needs to do. This process is called **gathering program requirements**. For example, if a customer wants a calculator program that adds two numbers together, the program needs to do three things. First, the user must be able to put two numbers into the program. Second, the two numbers must be accurately added together. Third, the program needs to display the answer. This is a simple example of a program's requirements.

Gathering program requirements usually involves meeting with the customer. Communicating and working together are very important in making sure a project is successful. If the program's requirements are clear, it is much easier to take the first step of coding—writing pseudocode.

It is important that everyone involved in a project understands all the requirements so that the program is successful. Organizing a list of must-haves, compared to things that would be nice to include, can help keep a project on track.

WHAT IS PSEUDOCODE?

Once all the programmers understand the requirements, they start outlining an **algorithm**. An algorithm is a plan for how a program will meet the specific program requirements. You may not realize it, but you already know some algorithms. In math, when you divide a large number, you're using an algorithm to solve that problem.

Once a general algorithm is chosen, the programmers start writing pseudocode. This method provides a simple way to write out an algorithm in plain English without having to worry about writing it in a computer coding language just yet. This lets programmers focus on each step of what the program needs to do. It also frees them from worrying about the very specific **syntax** (or structure) of a formal computer language.

COMPUTER CONNECTION

The word *algorithm* is a combination of the name of Muhammad ibn Mūsā al-Khwārizmī, who was a famous Persian mathematician, and the Greek word *arithmos*, meaning "number."

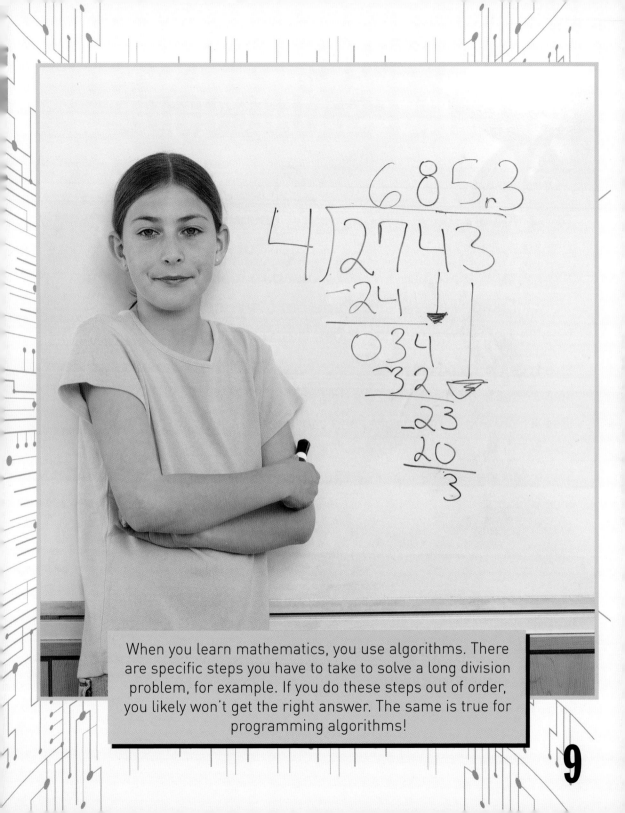

When you learn mathematics, you use algorithms. There are specific steps you have to take to solve a long division problem, for example. If you do these steps out of order, you likely won't get the right answer. The same is true for programming algorithms!

BAKING COOKIES WITH PSEUDOCODE

Pseudocode is all around us. A popular example programmers use when discussing pseudocode is baking cookies. If you've ever made or eaten cookies, a precise algorithm—the recipe—was followed to make sure the sweet treats baked properly and came out tasty. Here is what cookie pseudocode often looks like:

Step 1: Get a mixing bowl.

Step 2: Preheat the oven to 350 degrees.

Step 3: Put sugar, butter, eggs, and vanilla into a bowl.

Step 4: Put flour, salt, baking powder, and chocolate into a second bowl.

Step 5: Mix ingredients together to form dough.

Step 6: Scoop out the dough and place on a baking sheet.

Step 7: Bake in the oven for eight minutes.

Step 8: Remove from the oven and allow to cool. Enjoy!

This is a simple recipe, written in typical pseudocode style. It provides the instructions for baking delicious cookies.

COMPUTER CONNECTION

Computer scientists actually use the word "cookie" a lot! In their case, cookies are small files that hold information and details, such as a user's location or preferences, that the program remembers for the next time it is used.

If you've ever baked or cooked food, you probably know the importance of following a recipe. Sometimes the instructions are simple; sometimes they're more complex. But you usually get something delicious in the end!

GRAPHICAL PSEUDOCODE: PROGRAM DIAGRAMS

Baking cookies takes only a few steps, so the pseudocode is easy to write. But for more complicated projects, programmers need help writing all the pseudocode.

For complex projects, programmers use **diagrams**. Diagrams allow them to map out what a program will do. Diagrams are often written on a whiteboard or a notepad, but special computer tools can make diagramming easier.

EVENT-DRIVEN PROGRAMS

Programs that respond to user **interaction** are called event-driven programs. This means that users can click buttons, scroll down pages, or tap the screen, and the program will respond. Use-case diagrams are especially important for event-driven programs because they help programmers predict all the ways a user will try to interact with a program. Then the programmers can write code to handle each possibility.

For any electronic or digital game you play, a team of programmers has tried to predict all the moves you might make. They write code for all these scenarios on any device, such as a tablet or a virtual reality (VR) headset, that would support the game.

One type of diagram programmers use a lot is called a use-case diagram. It shows every possible way a user might interact with the program. Another example is a class diagram, which explains how different parts of code will need to interact with each other. Programmers use class diagrams to keep track of the overall project design and its components. Programmers look at these completed diagrams when they write the pseudocode.

WRITING THE FIRST SET OF PSEUDOCODE

After gathering program requirements, planning an algorithm, and drawing diagrams to guide the coding process, it's finally time to write pseudocode. That means creating a rough draft of the program in plain English—in other words, in the simplest terms possible. This first draft is usually written in a text document rather than in a coding program.

At this point, there's no need to use programming language syntax. However, it's helpful to stick to a general programming style, which means using the proper punctuation, **indentation**, and flow of how code is usually written. Once the rough draft is done in pseudocode, other programmers go through it to make any changes they think might be needed.

Each programming language has its own unique style. When programming in Java, for example, you have to include a semicolon at the end of each line of code. If you don't, the program will crash, meaning it will stop working until you fix the mistake.

```javascript
select();

ray_from_string(a) {
lace(/(\r\n|\n|\r)/gm, " ");
ceAll(",", " ", a);
lace(/ +(?= )/g, "");
split(" ");
    }
  $("#unique").click(function() {
    var a = array_from_string($("#fin").val
    if (c < 2 * b - 1) {
      return function("check" + c), this.t

    }
    for (b = 0;b < a.length;b++) {
      "" != a[b] && " " != a[b] || a.spli

    }
    b = $("#User_logged").val();
    array_from_string(b);
            length;b++) (c[b] =
```
15

MAKING CHANGES AND ADDING KEYWORDS

After the team reviews the rough draft, it is time to add **keywords** to the pseudocode. Keywords are special programming terms that control how a program will run. They are used only for specific **functions**. IF and ELSE are two examples of common keywords. They are used to make decisions, just as they are in real life: IF the cookies are done baking, you take them out of the oven, or ELSE you keep them in the oven a little bit longer. These two keywords help programmers control the flow of a program.

Adding keywords to the pseudocode rough draft provides the programmers with more information for when they're writing the final code.

COMPUTER CONNECTION

Programmers who use the keyword WHILE have to be very careful. If WHILE is used incorrectly, a program could get stuck and run for hundreds of years. It could even cause a computer to freeze!

16

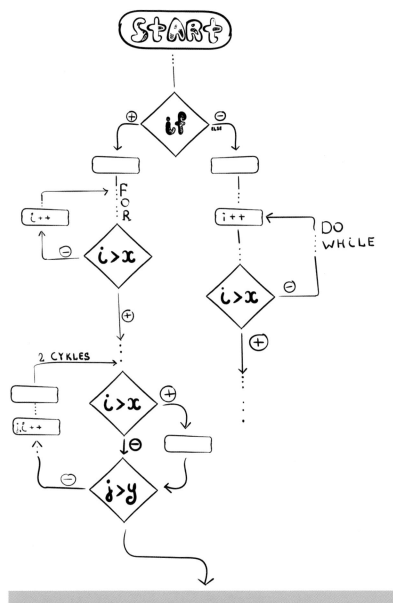

Keywords are used to direct the flow of a program.
A diagram like this, which includes keywords, helps
programmers understand how a program will operate.

ADDING LANGUAGE-SPECIFIC SYNTAX

After programmers add keywords, they take the next important step and add language syntax. While keywords give an idea of the algorithm's flow, syntax provides structure to the pseudocode. Adding syntax includes using proper indentation, such as if the code requires spaces on specific lines after using certain keywords (for example, WHILE, FOR, or IF).

PROGRAM LANGUAGE SYNTAX

Every coding language uses its own specific syntax rules, much like how sentences in English end with a period and have commas to separate clauses. Programmers have to learn these rules. Luckily, many coding languages share common syntax, which makes it easier to learn multiple languages. It's a lot like learning closely related languages, such as Spanish and Italian.

Computer programmers follow syntax rules when they are coding.

Placing related code into **blocks** helps group functions that are similar. Code blocks look a lot like paragraphs in a book. In many programming languages, blocks start and end with curly brackets. The brackets are an example of a **character** that programmers use to add more coding-language style. Syntax characters such as brackets ([ ]), curly brackets ({ }), and semicolons (;) make the pseudocode more formal. At this point, writing typically stops until all the pseudocode is reviewed and tested.

DOES YOUR ALGORITHM ACTUALLY WORK?

It's important to test that an algorithm is producing the correct results. All the programmers on a project spend hours reading through each line of pseudocode. They make sure every element is working as it should. This process is called code tracing.

During code tracing, programmers submit sample **input** into the program as a test. Then they trace—or keep track of—everything that would happen to the input by

COMPUTER CONNECTION
Mathematician Margaret Hamilton and her team wrote a huge amount of code for the Apollo space program in the 1960s. Even during a project as big as that one, Hamilton still checked her work—including when she rushed to her office one night after realizing a piece of code was flawed.

20

Computer programmers review output when they are code tracing.

going line by line through the pseudocode. Usually they use a piece of paper or a whiteboard to write down all the **outputs**—or results—from each line to make sure the algorithm is working.

If any issues come up, programmers change the pseudocode. Then they retrace the program to make sure the issues are fixed.

21

PSEUDOCODE AS COMMENTS IN THE FINAL PROGRAM

If all the pseudocode looks good and passes code-tracing tests, it's ready for the last step of the planning process. Programmers convert the pseudocode into **comments**. Comments are lines written in the final program that the computer does not read as code. They serve as plain English descriptions of what the code does, and they can help explain complex sections of code.

Comments are very helpful when new programmers are added to a project. Sometimes new programmers join a project after the planning and pseudocode-writing phases. Comments help them know what's going on. Comments can also clear up any confusion new programmers have. The best comments explain why the code was written a certain way, instead of just describing what the code is doing.

COMPUTER CONNECTION

Comments can also be used to create **documentation** for a project. Documentation acts as a manual for a program. It is often posted online so anyone who needs help using the program can read it.

Comments in a computer program are a lot like sticky notes you use to mark important text or further explain something you've read on paper.

23

WRITING THE FINAL PROGRAM CODE

After all that hard work planning and writing pseudocode, it's finally time to write real code. Programmers use their pseudocode and comments to carefully write the computer program. This process can take many forms. Sometimes one programmer writes the entire thing. But for larger projects, tasks are divided up among small groups of programmers. When all programmers complete their code, everything is put together as the final program.

The real code has to follow the proper syntax and style of the chosen programming language. It's important that programmers do not make any mistakes when translating their pseudocode into real code. A single error will cause the program to fail. One way to avoid making mistakes is by teaming up with a partner who can check the work. This is called **pair programming**.

PAIR PROGRAMMING

Two programmers with different skills and experience often pair up to work on a challenging project. Working with a partner to get a job done is very helpful and can reduce the number of errors in code. Pair programming improves the quality of the code, because the two are able to share ideas and select the best solutions to any problems.

Programmers often work on teams or in pairs, sometimes before they're even hired for a job. In a paired programming interview, the person interviewing for the job will program with the interviewer, giving both a realistic idea of how the candidate would perform in that role.

REFERENCING PSEUDOCODE AND DEBUGGING

Mistakes will happen, because no programmer is perfect. When the pseudocode has been converted to actual code, it's up to programmers to **debug**. Debugging is a fun term that means finding errors. For example, a program that's supposed to add two numbers together may return an incorrect answer, showing there's a bug.

Debugging can be difficult, especially if the bugs do not cause the program to fail. More complex errors require larger changes. Sometimes there are bugs in the flow of the program. These are called **logic errors**. They take a lot more work to fix and often require a look back at the original pseudocode. Logic errors do not cause the program to stop, so they may not be detected.

If a computer bug is not detected before a program is released, users will be frustrated when the program does not work properly. ❯

TECHNOLOGY ADVANCES MAKE CODING EASIER

Writing code is hard! It takes years of school, training, and practice for a programmer to be good at just one coding language. A lot of effort has been put into making coding easier. By removing difficult syntax requirements, languages such as Apple Swift let programmers quickly translate pseudocode into real code. These changes also allow programmers to test code more easily and to get completed programs out into the world faster.

LET'S GO!

The popular board game Go has been played for over two thousand years. Computer programmers wrote software that taught a computer (named AlphaGo) how to play. Programmers are working to teach computers human languages, games, and other skills that can be useful to us in the future.

If coding becomes easier, programs can be released into the world much more quickly.

Apple Swift and Python programming languages were built with the aim of making coding more natural and clearer for those reading it, much like how pseudocode is written. Natural language, which is how we write and speak to each other every day, is a favorite topic of research for computer scientists. They believe that if we can teach computers to understand everyday, natural language, it may be possible to have computers write their own code and perform actions automatically, without the need for code written in a formal computer language.

PSEUDOCODE: A HELPFUL TOOL FOR ALL PROGRAMMERS

Coding takes time, planning, and patience. Projects are more likely to succeed when programmers understand all the requirements and create diagrams to guide the process. Turning these diagrams into pseudocode allows programmers to get their ideas onto paper and then test them for bugs. Leaving comments in pseudocode helps orient everyone on the project so they know what the code does and why.

Fully developed pseudocode is vital to programmers because it keeps them organized as they write. It also makes coding much simpler. It's an essential step in the fun, challenging, exciting process of computer programming. For programmers, pseudocode is the road map they consult if they have questions. It's the critical link between a cool, new idea and the final code that will run your favorite program.

GLOSSARY

algorithm: A step-by-step method for solving a problem.

block: A way to organize code into related sections.

character: A printed or written letter or symbol.

coding language: A computer language designed to give instructions to a computer.

comment: A note left by a programmer that describes what code does.

debug: The process of finding and removing errors that cause code to fail.

diagram: A drawing that explains or shows the parts of something or how something works.

documentation: A detailed manual for users written by programmers.

function: A task that something or someone performs.

gathering program requirements: The act of understanding what a program needs to do.

indentation: A space or many spaces used at the start of a line to add structure.

input: Information that is entered into a computer.

interaction: When two things communicate with each other or are used by each other.

keyword: A reserved word that has a special function in computer programming.

logic error: A mistake that produces the incorrect result but does not cause a program to stop.

output: The result of a program's being run.

pair programming: When two programmers work together on the same code.

pseudocode: Instructions for a computer written in everyday language, rather than coding language.

syntax: The formal rules of a computer programming language that programmers need to follow.

INDEX

WEBSITES

Due to the changing nature of Internet links, PowerKids Press has developed an online list of websites related to the subject of this book. This site is updated regularly. Please use this link to access the list: www.powerkidslinks.com/eccs/pseudo